Date: 4/26/17

J BIO NAVARRO
Juarez, Christine,
José Antonio Navarro /

D1226789

Pebble®

GREAT HISPANIC AND LATINO AMERICANS

José Antonio Navarro

by Christine Juarez

Consultant: M. M. McAllen, Adjunct Professor of History
University of Texas at San Antonio

CAPSTONE PRESS
a capstone imprint

Pebble Books are published by Capstone Press,
1710 Roe Crest Drive, North Mankato, Minnesota 56003
www.mycapstone.com

Library of Congress Cataloging-in-Publication Data
Names: Juarez, Christine, 1976–
Title: José Antonio Navarro / by Christine Juarez.
Description: North Mankato, Minnesota : Capstone Press, 2017.
| Series: Pebble books. Great Hispanic and Latino Americans | Includes
bibliographical references and index.
Identifiers: LCCN 2016003660| ISBN 9781515718895 (library binding) |
ISBN 9781515719007 (paperback) | ISBN 9781515719205 (eBook pdf)
Subjects: LCSH: Navarro, José Antonio, 1795–1871—Juvenile literature.|
Statesmen—Texas—Biography—Juvenile literature. | Mexican Americans—
Texas—Biography—Juvenile literature. | Texas—History—Revolution, 1835–1836—
Juvenile literature. | Texas—History—Republic, 1836–1846—Juvenile literature.
Classification: LCC F390.N38 J83 2017 | DDC 976.4/03092—dc23
LC record available at http://lccn.loc.gov/2016003660

Note to Parents and Teachers

The Great Hispanic and Latino Americans series supports national
curriculum standards for social studies related to people, places,
and culture. This book describes and illustrates José Antonio
Navarro. The images support early readers in understanding
the text. The repetition of words and phrases helps early readers
learn new words. This book also introduces early readers to
subject-specific vocabulary words, which are defined in the
Glossary section. Early readers may need assistance to read some
words and to use the Table of Contents, Glossary, Read More,
Internet Sites, and Index sections of the book.

Printed in the United States of America in North Mankato, Minnesota.
009663F16

Table of Contents

a statue of José Antonio Navarro in San Antonio

1795
born

Early Years

José Antonio Navarro was
an important leader in Texas.
He was born February 27, 1795,
in San Antonio, Texas.
At this time, Texas was not
part of the United States.

San Antonio in the 1800s

1795
born

1808
leaves
school to
help family

José's father, Angel Navarro, died in 1808. Young José was going to school in Mexico. He left school to help his family back at home.

1795
born

1808
leaves
school to
help family

The Spanish army took over San Antonio in 1813. José and his family were against Spain. They had to go to the U.S. state of Louisiana for safety.

San Antonio military plaza in the early 1800s

1795
born

1808
leaves school to help family

1816
goes back to Texas

Adulthood

In 1816 José went back to Texas.
He made money trading horses
and goods. By 1821 Mexico
was in charge of Texas.
José was chosen to represent
Texas in Mexico's government.

Stephen F. Austin

1795
born

1808
leaves school to help family

1816
goes back to Texas

José became friends with American Stephen F. Austin. Austin had arrived in 1821. He settled 300 American families in Texas. José began to think about Texas joining the United States.

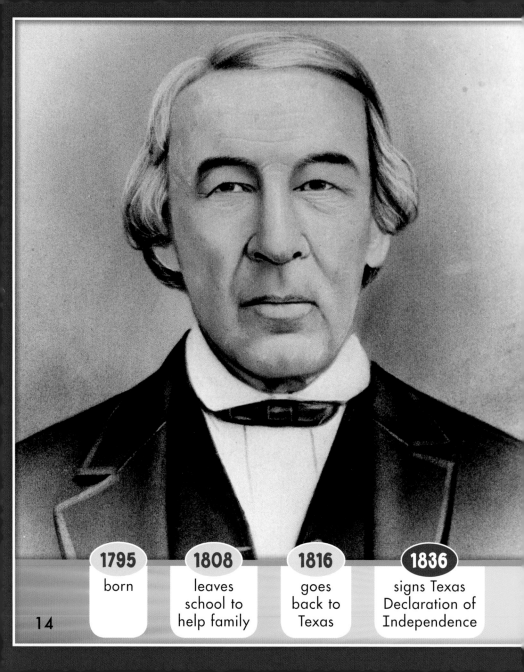

| 1795 | 1808 | 1816 | 1836 |
| born | leaves school to help family | goes back to Texas | signs Texas Declaration of Independence |

In 1836 José was one of three Mexicans to sign the Texas Declaration of Independence. It called for Texas to be free from Mexico.

official ceremony that made Texas the 28th U.S. state

1795
born

1808
leaves school to help family

1816
goes back to Texas

1836
signs Texas Declaration of Independence

In 1845 José voted for Texas to become a U.S. state. He made sure the new state's constitution did not leave out Tejanos. He said they should have the same rights as white Texans.

Tejano: a Texan of Hispanic background

1845
votes for Texas
to become a
U.S. state

1795
born

1808
leaves
school to
help family

1816
goes
back to
Texas

1836
signs Texas
Declaration of
Independence

José served in the first

Texas state senate

from 1846 to 1848.

He kept working for

the rights of Tejanos.

1845
votes for Texas
to become a
U.S. state

1846-1848
serves in
first Texas
state senate

José's home in San Antonio

1795	1808	1816	1836
born	leaves school to help family	goes back to Texas	signs Texas Declaration of Independence

Remembering José

José died January 13, 1871.

Today, people can visit

his home in San Antonio.

They learn about the life of

this Texas patriot.

1845	**1846-1848**	**1871**
votes for Texas to become a U.S. state	serves in first Texas state senate	dies

Glossary

army—a group of soldiers trained to fight on land

constitution—a document that explains the system of laws and government in a state or country

government—the group of people who make laws, rules, and decisions for a country or state

independence—freedom

patriot—a person who loves and fights for his or her country or homeland

right—something one can or must do by law

senate—a part of government that helps make laws

Read More

Gibson, Karen Bush. *Texas History for Kids: Lone Star Lives and Legends*. Chicago: Chicago Review Press, 2015.

Peppas, Lynn. *Why José Antonio Navarro Matters to Texas*. Texas Perspectives. New York: Rosen Publishing Group, Inc., 2014.

Internet Sites

FactHound offers a safe, fun way to find Internet sites related to this book. All of the sites on FactHound have been researched by our staff.

Here's all you do:

Visit *www.facthound.com*

Type in this code: 9781515718895

Check out projects, games and lots more at
www.capstonekids.com

Index

Editorial Credits

Erika L. Shores, editor; Charmaine Whitman, designer;
Kelly Garvin, media researcher; Tori Abraham, production specialist

Photo Credits

Alamy: Niday Picture Library, 12, Pat Eyre, 20, Witold Skrypczak, 4; Corbis/AS400-DB/Bettmann, 10; Daughters of the Republic of Texas Library/SC96_247, copy of crayon portrait, Alamo Collection, cover, 1, 14; North Wind Picture Archive, 6; Texas Historical Commission, 18; Texas State Library and Archives Commission, 8, 16
Artistic Elements: Shutterstock: Eliks, nalinn, tuulijumala